CHRIS MARTIN
BOOK MAKER

Copyright © 2025 Chris Martin

All rights reserved. No part of this book may be reproduced, stored in a retrieval system, or transmitted in any form or by any means, electronic, mechanical, photocopying, recording, or otherwise, without prior written permission from the copyright holder, except for brief excerpts used in reviews or for educational purposes.

For permission requests, contact:

Chris Martin

Email: booksmakeroffice@gmail.com

You are allowed to rest.

Thoughts pass — you remain.

You are whole, even in pieces.

Both light and shadow are part of you.

Let go, flow, become.

You are infinite.

Keep moving forward, gently.

Savor this pause — it's yours.

You are blooming, even on quiet days.

Inhale peace, exhale fear.

Take your time. It's yours.

Beauty grows in unexpected places.

Choose kindness — always.

Grow thoughts that serve you.

Your truth is beautiful.

You are stronger than you think.

Peace begins within.

You carry galaxies within.

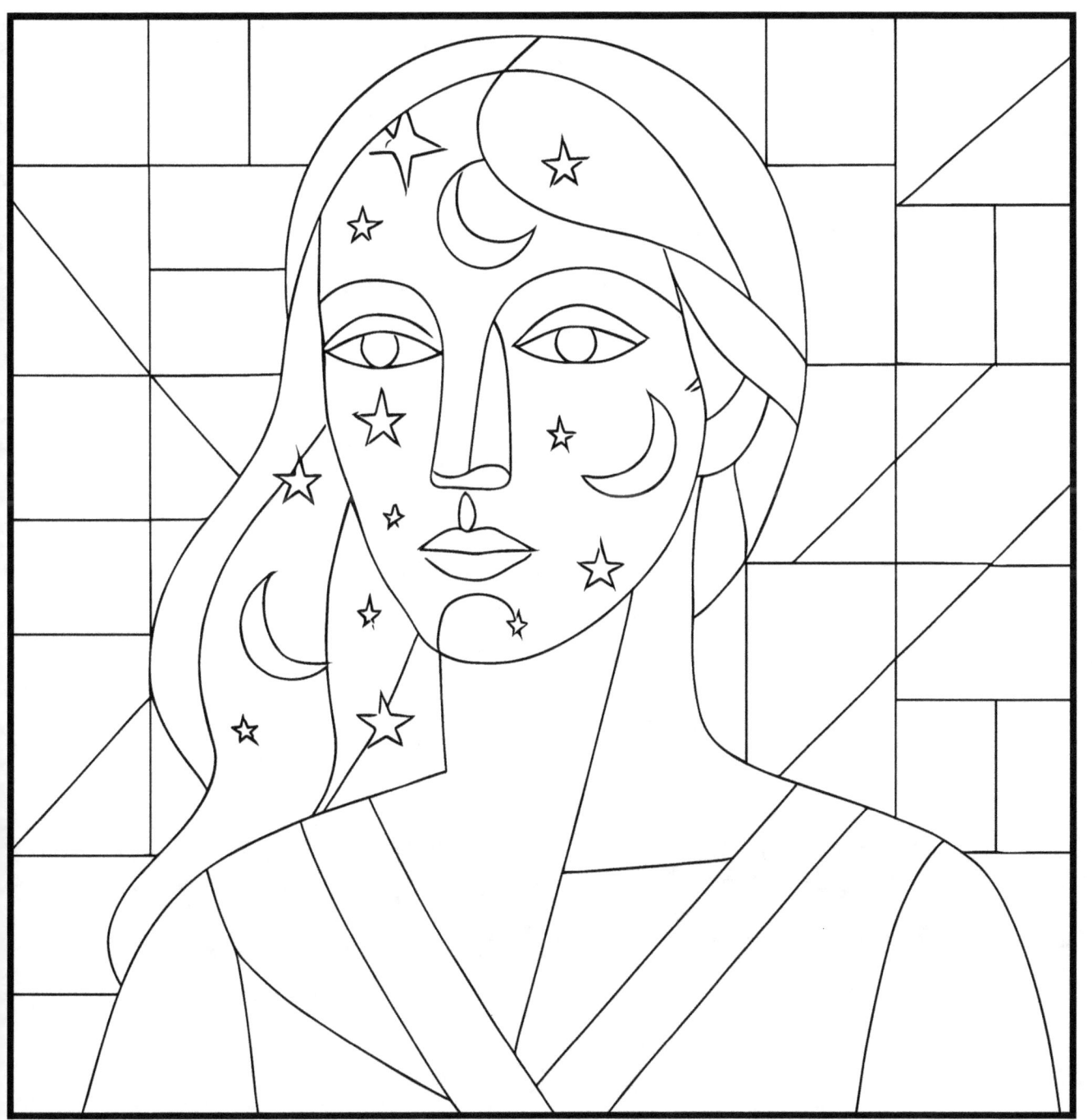

Your light matters.

There is grace in imperfection.

Set your thoughts free.

Balance is a form of strength.

You are your own safe space

Transform gently, grow boldly.

Feed your mind, free your soul.

Dreams begin in stillness.

Joy needs no permission.

You are who you are.

Hold space for your dreams.

All your emotions are valid.

www.ingramcontent.com/pod-product-compliance
Lightning Source LLC
LaVergne TN
LVHW060217080526
838202LV00052B/4294